When Someone You Know Dies
And You Need To Tell A Child

Remember our Angels

Roberta Andresen

This book is dedicated to my son Wally, whose untimely death at the age of 26 gave reason and a need for a book like this. I shall do as much good in this world as I can in his memory.

"We all miss you so very much!"

My Daddy Died

Roberta Andresen

Illustrated by Tim O'Leary

Andresen Enterprises
57 Richmond Street, Raynham, MA 02767
U.S.A.

ACKNOWLEDGEMENTS

I would like to acknowledge the many sacrifices and valuable time given to my grandchildren by "Uncle Matt". He is solely responsible for filling the tremendous void left by the death of my son Wally. He is a treasure to every member of my family.

Many thanks and deep appreciation to all Wally's friends who have done so much to keep his memory among us. I receive my greatest joy and pride from all that you do.

A special thought for Werner, the one who encouraged me to begin and then complete this story.

Cassandra - my little "best friend" who brings such pleasure to my troubled world.

And now, a special thank you to my dearest Angel in heaven, Wally, who I know guided every thought and word written.

* A special donation will be given to the American Cancer Society in honor of each person who purchases this book.

Together, we WILL make a difference.

Andresen Enterprises
57 Richmond Street
Raynham, MA 02767 U.S.A.
(508) 821-2550
Fax (508) 821-2550

Library of Congress Catalog Card Number: 94-96716

ISBN: 0-9641718-0-5

Printed in the United States of America

This book is based on the author's practical personal experience and does not purport to provide psychological counseling.

Table of Contents

Author's Note

This story describes how to explain death effectively to children. It explains the separation between body and soul/spirit in a way that a child can effectively understand and deal with the process. It gives knowledge of the afterlife, of the funeral rites, and a meaningful way to say good-bye, which helps to accept the finality of death.

This total guide in dealing with death and children has been proven to work completely. This story uses examples that will prevent most of the fear associated with death and describes a way to express love for the deceased that brings peace and happiness to a child.

A must for such a vulnerable time.

FORWARD

Do you recall your first experience with death? Was it the death of someone close to you, or a distant relative that you hardly knew, or was it one of your parents? Do you recall how you felt upon hearing such news? If you do , then you will have strong feelings about the title of this book, MY DADDY DIED.

This story is about the most heartbreaking event my family has ever had to deal with - the illness and death of my oldest son, Walter. We looked for guidance to help us deal effectively with his two small children so that the trauma of their first encounter with a "death experience" would not scar them for life. We found very little that was simple and appropriate for their age. After my unsuccessful search for something helpful, I decided to draw from my own knowledge and experience. The results were so positive that I decided to share our experiences in hopes that we can help many others who find themselves in similiar circumstances. This is how this book came to be.

As my grandchildren faced their first encounter with a "death experience", my main concern was knowing how and what to say to the children. When you read about their experiences, it should give you ideas on how to effectively explain death and the rituals that follow to any child facing the loss of a loved one. During their first personal involvement with death, a child will learn a lot of new facts and they must be reliable. This is necessary in order to prevent lifelong emotional scars and to allow the eventual acceptance of the finality of death.

Facing death is difficult for anyone, but even more so for a child. How are they supposed to begin to cope or adjust to death when they have had no preparation for this in their normal daily life? Children need a great deal of help to understand what is normal and natural as a result of seeing and feeling what I refer to as a "death experience". They need to know that the sadness they feel is normal and so are the feelings of anger, loss, hurt and separation. A child may also show signs of physical illness or even some denial about the whole situation.

It is easy for grieving adults to forget children. Try not to let this happen. Include them in as much of the preparations and rituals as possible. They are people too and need as much, if not more, help and understanding. Damaging psychological defenses can occur if a child is thrown into a "death experience" without help and guidance. These defenses are capable of interrupting the emotional growth of any child. Children need to be given tools to help them overcome and cope with the situation and then taught how to put them to use. Most of all they need understanding. Give them plenty of attention in a way that they feel free to express their new emotions. Try and remember back to when you first learned of death.

How comfortable were you with the way you were told about your first loss of a loved one and did it affect your life in any way?

I can not stress enough the need for more discussions concerning the subject of death in our society. If we talked more about it, we would develop an awareness and a beginning for our understanding of this basic normal process of life. A death crisis should be shared by all the members of a family together, and if possible, include the help from close friends. This sharing and caring gives comfort to those left to mourn. Death is something that most everyone fears but it must not be that way. There are certain facts that are reliable in understanding the subject and we should be exposed to these early in life. Try not to wait until your child is personally involved before you begin discussing them. It is very difficult to combine grief with learning about something new. Don't be afraid. There are two things that everyone can be sure of in their lifetime. One is their own birth and the other is their own death. Every member of our entire family before us has experienced both events but so little information has been passed to us especially about the death. We celebrate the birth with great joy and enthusiasm while death is among the subjects considered by everyone as TABOO.

Remember to talk to the children about how their lives will change in the future following the loss of a loved one. Talk openly about what it will be like to NOT have that special person around celebrating important occasions or just your everyday events in life. Many times other children will bring up the subject of the missing person so prepare your child with ways to answer them ahead of time. This subject of how their lives will be different without that special person should wait until after the funeral except when the children ask. If this is discussed before the loved one is placed in his or her final resting place, the child may feel a degree of guilt. Thinking of alternatives to life without that certain someone can be very painful. The people in our lives are very precious to us and the earlier we learn that lesson the more happiness we will have and less regrets when a loved one dies.

Grieving adults, as I said, can overlook a great deal. Don't. Try to help the children begin a normal period of recovery right away. It has been mentioned that history sometimes repeats itself. In my case, I lost my father at about the same age as my grandchildren lost their father. At that time no one tried to help any of my siblings or me through that painful ordeal. Society thought that children could be brushed aside. We have found out differently. As a result, my siblings and I carry life-long scars. I decided to change this for my grandchildren.

The illustrator of this book was chosen from among many applicants. Tim had reason to be emotionally involved with this project. His Mother died from a form of lymphoma cancer in 1991 leaving Tim and younger siblings. When he read my story, he said, "We could have used a book like this at the time of my Mother's death." So together we have tried to help so many others that will find themselves in similar situations. I put my heart into this story and you will see that he put his heart into the illustrations. Thank you, Tim.

Also I would like to mention that the front cover of the book was designed by my grandson Nathan Loveday, as a result of wanting to help with this project. He said the memory of sending up the balloons was the best part for him. At the time he felt he was helping the Angels bring Daddy's spirit to heaven. What a nice memory to keep in a heart of a seven year old boy.

The following story should now be read to any child facing their first "death experience". In reading this story, you will find that it explains the concept, process, and rituals of death clearly and can be applied to the loss of any loved one.

I would like to express my sincere gratitude to Nathan and Ashley for letting me tell their story in such a way that it would help all those who have to experience a loss of a loved one through death. The more we shared our emotions, the more I realized that a story like this is so tremendously needed in the world of grief.

"We will now let the Angels do their jobs."

My Daddy Died

In my Grandmama's home there was a large collection of Cherubs and Angels surrounding the many items that she held dear to her. Little did I know growing up that these Cherubs would become the link between my intense personal pain and the beginning of a lifelong healing process over the death of my father.

I would often ask my Grandmama why she had so many Cherubs and Angels. They were hanging on the walls, sitting near the glassware on the mantel, and perched upon the grandfather clock. Their positions allowed them to blow kisses to everyone that passed. Her explanation was quick and always with a smile of how one day she actually saw "Angels" and "Cherubs" floating alongside her as she traveled through a tunnel towards a bright light. You see, one day my Grandmama was

diagnosed with cancer and had to undergo major surgery that lasted 11 hours. During this time she had serious problems and her heart stopped . This phenomenon has been referred to by many before, but never by anyone that I had known personally. This is where she saw for the first time the beautiful babies which we refer to as the "Angels" and "Cherubs" of heaven. Her first thought was "wow - they really do exist."

The ones referred to as Cherubs only have heads with wings, while the Angels have whole bodies with wings. They all sang the most beautiful songs that she had ever heard. As they sang, these beautiful little babies floated alongside Grandmama towards a bright light which appeared at the end of the tunnel. While she was floating upward, Grandmama could look down and see her body on the bed below. Here she could stay for awhile as she watched and heard those around her frantically working hard to revive her. As the pain totally left her body, Grandmama was closer to the bright light. As she came to the end of the tunnel, she stood alone. Then with her mind and not her lips to do the talking, she discussed her whole life as it flashed before her. The part that stands out the most in her memory is the part where she understood how each person felt as a result of what she had done to them. When Grandmama talks about this special event, she has such a peaceful look in her eyes and a longing to experience it once more.

As she finished looking at all the events of her life, from birth to the present, something strange took place. This was the fact she was given the opportunity to go back down into her earthly body again. At first she did not want to return and leave such warmth and pure love, but, finally she did make the decision to return. And as she floated back down through the tunnel of light, she began to experience again the intense pain of the surgery. Following this episode, she knew that her life would be altogether different from before, both in her thinking and in her decision making, because she survived this "near death" experience.

My Grandmama kept this occurrence quiet for many years until one day she heard that someone else had had a similar experience and wrote a book about it. In the meantime her collection of "Angels" and the "Cherubs" started to exist. This collection was my introduction to the cherished ones that I believe carried the spirit of my father all the way to heaven. Only my Daddy didn't have the opportunity or chance to come back because his earthly body was no longer habitable. Apparently it was his time to die.

I can remember being called together with my little sister so that my Uncle Matt and

Grandmama could tell us what was happening to our Daddy. My Daddy had cancer. This frightened me a lot because I didn't know if he would live or die. In my mind he was too young to die and besides, he had us to take care of. Up until this point in my life, I had not experienced anyone's dying. I was not quite sure what it meant to die, let alone someone I loved so much. Of course I knew that when you stepped on a bug it died and didn't get up, but I wasn't sure what real people did. I saw that sometimes in the movies people that are supposed to be dead get up again and sometimes they even come out of the grave and scare you. But for me, I had no real idea what this thing called DEATH meant as far as what would actually happen to someone I loved.

Grandmama and Uncle Matt sat with my little sister and me on the couch. I can still feel Uncle Matt's strong arm around me holding me close while Grandmama held my little hand in hers. I trusted both of them and knew that what they would tell us would be the truth. The last time that I saw my Daddy he was very sick and that scared me. He didn't look the same and he smelled differently from what I was used to. I loved him so much that all this confused me. Then I started to believe that I could make this whole situation go away if I thought about it hard enough. But I was wrong.

Grandmama's voice was calm and steady as she began with what she needed to tell us. "Daddy is awfully sick and his body will not be able to keep going much longer." "Daddy will be ready very soon to go to heaven." "The Angels will come and together they will hold Daddy's spirit in their arms and float him to heaven where he will feel no more pain." My sister and I began to cry but Grandmama kept her voice calm and steady as she explained to us what this meant. The first thing that I needed to know at that moment was what was Daddy's spirit? Will he float like magic up to the sky? Just what was going to happen?

"Well," she said, "close your eyes and think about being away somewhere while Daddy is here sick. What do you think about him? What do you remember about him?" I thought about it for only a few minutes and said, "I think about his voice talking to me, and I think about the times that he played ball with me, and I think about going fishing with him and how he would help me put the worms on the hooks. I think about how I feel good inside of me that I have a Daddy that loves me so much." Grandmama asked me if I could see what he looks like? "Yes," I said, "I can think about what he looks like." "Well," she said, "all this is what makes up the spirit of your Daddy. All the things that he did and all the feelings that he showed, along with what he

looks like to us in our memories, makes up what his spirit is. This is what the Angels and the Cherubs will carry up to heaven. The body that your Daddy used while on earth doesn't work any more and so something special will take place with it so that it doesn't cause any harm to anyone. We will take good care of it and see to it that it is put in a very special place. We do this because we loved this body so much when Daddy's spirit was in it."

Grandmama told us that things would change for all of us very soon, but we should remember that the love we felt for our Daddy will remain in our hearts always. We could sense that something very serious was happening. I felt relieved when Grandmama told us about what to expect rather than what my child's imagination was creating deep inside my hidden thoughts. I knew God would like having my Daddy in heaven. He was so much fun down here for everyone, but at the same time I felt very sad and the tears started streaming down my cheeks. It's okay to cry. "Sadness makes us want to cry sometimes," she said. Just then I could see that Grandmama was crying just like me. This seemed to give my little sister the feeling that it was okay to cry and that we didn't need to hold it all in.

Now it was my time to talk about what was happening if I wanted to. Grandmama asked me if I had any special thoughts about Daddy and what

was going to take place very soon. I thought at first someone might be mad at me for thinking that it would not be so bad if Daddy died, because then he would not have all the bad pain that made him so sick. But no one was mad at me for thinking that. In fact, everyone said that they didn't want to see Daddy suffer any longer. This made me feel okay about what I said. At the same time I was thinking that I was very glad that I went to the hospital with Daddy and watched the doctors give him chemotherapy. Chemotherapy is a very strong medicine the doctors give people that have cancer with the hopes that it will kill the cancer cells. I knew that they tried to cure my Daddy's cancer, but that the final decision was out of their hands. While being around Daddy most of the time that he was sick, I learned that everyone can do some things, and NOT others in order to take good care of their own health. I felt confused and I wondered why so many grown-ups were doing things that I learned would cause cancer. There would be times I would be in the same room with different grown-ups, all who were smoking, and I would be so afraid that their smoke could make me have cancer and die like Daddy. Sometimes I would hold my breath in the car when there was too much cigarette smoke. Little did I know at that time "secondhand smoke DOES kill indeed!" I often would hear grown-ups say,

"Well, if only I could stop smoking." My advice should have been, "Well - try getting CANCER, it stops you from smoking real quick."

So as we sat together on the sofa, we all knew the one thing that we were so afraid of was going to take place. Our Daddy really was going to die and it would be very soon. Grandmama reached over and picked up two of her small white angels from the coffee table and gave one to each of us. "Let's put these in the room near Daddy so they will help him get ready to go to heaven." I picked up mine and held it in my hand, then went into the bedroom and placed it on the headboard near the only light in the room - a glowing candle. Here it would sit and wait until the real angels would come and carry Daddy's spirit to heaven for good. Grandmama also reminded us that everyone is born and that everyone will die. It doesn't matter if you are young or old, good or bad, big or small. God is the only force that controls the when and how this will all take place. But, we must remember that we have been promised by HIM that someday we will all be together again. As each one of us dies, we will join those that have gone before us. Then we leaned over and kissed Daddy on the cheek, which turned out to be for the last time. Then we went home. I called the next day and asked if the Angels and Cherubs had come for Daddy yet? I was told no. Two days later

Uncle Matt and Grandmama came to our house and told us that the Angels had come that afternoon. Daddy was now in heaven with all the other Angels and Cherubs. I cried so hard, but at the same time I knew that I would see him again. The next time he would not be in so much pain.

My sister and I felt that our heartache was more than we could bear. But at the same time we had some questions about all that was happening. Where is Daddy's body now Grandmama? Did the Angels take it to heaven also? "No," she said, "that part of Daddy didn't work right anymore and we need to do something special with it. You see, when the spirit leaves the body and goes to heaven, the body becomes something that we can't use any more. It only had one purpose and that was to let the spirit of Daddy live inside it until it was time for the spirit to go to heaven. There are special people that have the job to take care of this task. They are called Funeral Directors or Undertakers. Their job is to take good care of all the special bodies that used to have a spirit in them. By law, they must take the body to where they work and get it ready for whatever the family decides to do at that time. The family can do two things only. One is to have a special time that everyone who loved that person when he/she was alive could come and see it for the last time. Here prayers would be said so that the

Angels taking care of the spirit in heaven will do an extra special job at it and prayers are also said so that God will give the spirit eternal peace. And the other is that, maybe, the family will decide to have it made into ashes by a process called cremation. The ashes would then be put in a very special container that will be placed somewhere for safe keeping." I had never heard of any of this before and I truly wondered how this would all work out.

Grandmama said that we needed to take out our best clothes to wear. This was to show respect for the occasion. Also, we should think about something special that we wanted to bring to our Daddy to keep with his body forever. I thought of bringing a hockey puck and a picture of Daddy and me playing hockey. I also wanted to write a letter to Daddy telling him how much I loved him and would miss him. My Mother helped me get all this ready. She then asked Ashley what she thought would be her idea of something special. Ashley decided to draw a picture and make a card for Daddy. She likes to draw a lot and Mom helped her write some nice words on the inside. Now we were all ready for what would take place next.

We had to wait for the next day to be told that Daddy's body was ready for us to see. Grandmama explained that all his friends would come and say goodbye to his body. We were going to the Funeral

Home where Daddy would be in a special box called a casket. The Funeral Home is the place where the special handling of a body is done. Daddy would be wearing his best clothes just like us and he would have his hands folded on his chest. Remember that we all loved Daddy very much, but the part of him that is in our hearts and in our memory has been taken up to heaven. We will be looking at only the body that held Daddy's spirit while he was alive with us. The funeral people will take very special care to make Daddy look like he did before he got so sick with cancer. They may put some powder on his face or color on his lips. They may even comb his hair a special way. They really do a good job at this so that we can remember more of the good times rather than the time when Daddy was very sick. We are also going to send flowers to the Funeral Home so that Daddy will know that he was very special. This would be like the flowers we may send on birthdays and other special occasions.

The day came when we were all ready to go to what was referred to as visiting hours. These are the hours set aside for family and friends to visit the body at the Funeral Home. As we walked into the the Funeral Home, Mommie reminded us that we still could change our minds and not go in to see Daddy's body. Ashley and I didn't want to change our minds. We went in and saw the body of Daddy lying in a beautiful casket. To us his body looked okay. It didn't look anything like what it did when he was very sick and in so much pain. This alone made me feel that it was better for Daddy to be in heaven rather than in his bed suffering with so much pain. I noticed Grandmama had made a pin with our pictures on it and put it on his suit. It also made me feel good to see several of Daddy's pictures displayed around the room. I noticed one was of Daddy with us and one was just of Daddy as a little boy.

Going through all this was very frightening to both my sister and me. We were comforted by being surrounded by all the people that I knew were strong and many that already helped us during our lives. I could see Grandmama standing close with my Uncle Matt. I knew right away that if I needed them, they would be right there to help. When Uncle Matt came over to me and gave me a squeeze on my shoulder, it made me feel strong . All this made it possible for me to face, for the first time in my life, a body that the spirit or soul has gone out of it. As I look back on this experience, I feel that a child's impression of death is usually so far from actual reality that most times it is hard to undo the damage of what some stories and movies have led them to believe. And I feel that this is very sad. Maybe my story will help give the impression that death, although very sad, is a real part of life .

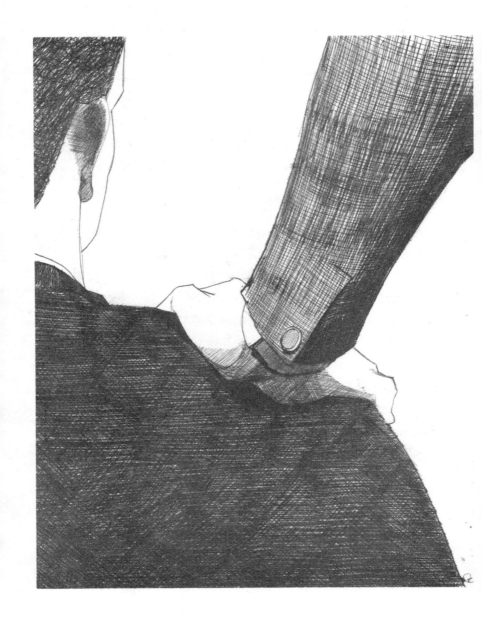

My sister and I walked up to the casket together with our special mementos in our hands. We knelt down together on the kneeler placed in front of the casket and looked at our Daddy. I wanted so much to cry but the tears would not come out. I wanted so much to scream at Daddy to get up and act like my real Daddy again and hold me. I also knew this could not happen. My Grandmama did such a wonderful job in explaining to us that our Daddy was with the Angels now and not really in that big box called a casket. I could actually visualize in my mind that I was looking at only the body that held my Daddy. I wanted so much for everyone to take special care of it. I wanted so much to put something beside it so that Daddy could see that I cared about his body. I was so glad that I had my special picture in my hand. Carefully I reached over and laid it down beside his hands. No one moved it from that spot the whole time that everyone was coming to look at my Daddy's body. My sister had trouble reaching so far, so I helped her do it. She was also happy to give something special to Daddy's body. She wanted to show him how much she loved him also. I now felt at peace inside myself and I was ready to leave. Mommie quickly said good-by with us and we walked out of the room and went home. I knew that we would come back on the day that they would take my father's body to a new place for safekeeping.

For the next few days everything in our house was very hectic. Everyone was coming over to tell us that they were sorry that my Daddy died. I felt very sad most of the time and this sad feeling would come in a very strong way just before I would have to go to bed. It seems that every time there is a situation, both good or bad, I would think mostly about it just before I fell asleep at night. So at this time, the sadness would come and make me feel sick all over. My chest would feel very heavy and ache while my stomach would feel sick. There would be times when I would be overwhelmed with the idea that maybe I would get sick also. Sometimes I would feel that maybe I was going to die just like my Daddy, because we were so close and did everything the same. Grandmama always said that I looked like and walked just like my Dad so, maybe, there was a chance it could happen to me. I was so glad when my Mommie told me that this would NOT happen to me. Just because someone in your life dies, it does not mean that you are going to die also. I needed to hear this and when I did, it made me feel better.

When I cried, I would feel worse like I had a very bad flu, but then the pressure in me would be a little easier to handle. Everyone said that it was good for me to cry. Crying was necessary at a time like this. It is a physical release of our very sad emotions. I was told by Grandmama that crying

emotions. I was told by Grandmama that crying was not a sign of weakness but rather an expression of the inexpressible pain of separation from someone you love. This is exactly what I felt but didn't know how to put it into words for myself. I also was told that if I felt sick, it was a normal reaction to such a great loss in my life. I remember that specific words didn't mean as much as the tone of voice used, which was warm, sympathetic and kind. What is said is significant, but "how" it is said will have a greater bearing on whether a child accepts death or develops unnecessary fears about death. I can remember that my little sister showed a type of indifference to the death of Daddy but now I understand that this had to do with her age and ability to cope with loss. I do not think that she could handle everything at once. Nor could I, but two years between us made the difference for me.

The day had arrived. This is the day that they would do something special with the body of my Daddy. Grandmama came over to talk to us once more. She was always good at doing that. She always let us feel that we could tell her how we felt also. Nothing I could say would shake her up, even though sometimes I would try. Grandmama wanted to explain to us what was going to take place today so that we would not wonder and make up something in our minds that would frighten us. She said

44

that we would all gather at the Funeral Home for the last time to sit with the body of Daddy. We would say some prayers that would ask God to grant special peace to the soul of Daddy. And at some point, there would be someone to say a special tribute or "eulogy" about how Daddy touched each of our lives. Grandmama said she would be the one to say the "eulogy". If there was something special that my sister or I wanted her to say either to Daddy or about Daddy, we could let her know. She made us feel involved in all that was happening. It would have been dreadful to have been excluded at this time because we felt we were the ones closest to him in his life. We were not forced to go to any of the events but were asked and then included. That was fine with me. Grandmama told us that the casket would be closed for the last time and brought to a church where a Service would be said for Daddy. For us this meant a Mass. This is where the "eulogy" would be said. From here the body of Daddy, in the casket, would be brought by a long slow procession of cars containing friends and family to the cemetery. Here the casket would be placed in a special location called a grave that would hold and take care of Daddy's body until the end of time. She explained to us that the law requires all bodies that have not been cremated are to be buried in the ground where someone will protect it for as many years as we are

on this earth. This sounded good to me because I didn't want anyone to disturb my Daddy's body ever.

This is the most special part of all. My Grandmama had helium-filled balloons that were red and white which said "I Love you Daddy" on them delivered to the cemetery. She told us that we would each be given one. We were to kiss it and then hand it to the Angels who would scoop up Daddy's spirit and take it to heaven for the last time. We were so happy to feel that we could be a part of that. When the time came for us to do this, I remember being proud that I was actually going to help the Angels take Daddy's spirit to heaven. I remember that my sister and I NEVER looked down. We did not think of our Daddy going anywhere but up. We did not need to ask the question of where is Daddy now. You see, all along, right from the moment my Daddy died until the time that his body was placed in the ground for safekeeping, we were told what was happening and why it was happening. We were always given the chance to ask our questions and to express our feelings. Grandmama said that the expression of our hurt and sad emotions was good, and that the suppression of them was harmful and could be very bad for us in our future lives. And now on each occasion that we want to remember or send a gift to our Daddy, we send him a bouquet of

48

helium balloons. We release and watch them float straight up to heaven where the spirit of Daddy is now. This lets us feel that we still can communicate with him and that he knows what our hearts are trying to say .

Many years have passed since the time of Daddy's death, but the memory I have of it seems so very real to me at certain moments. There have been occasions on my birthday, Christmas, or on the anniversary of the day that he died, I feel painful feelings of severe loss. Sometimes they last for a short time, sometimes they last for longer periods of time. But deep inside my heart, I know that my spirit will join Daddy one day. I am very much looking forward to this wonderful moment. I truly believe that this will happen at the end of my lifetime, because you see, I believe all that Grandmama did and said to us at the time surrounding the death of my Daddy. But what is more important, I believe in the "Angels".

"Don't you?"

Do you have friends or relatives who would like to have copies of this book? If so, please fill out the order blank below or call to order.

ORDER FORM

Please send _____ copies of MY DADDY DIED at $6.95 each to:

Name _____

Address _____

City _____ State _____ Zip _____

Telephone (_____) _____

Method of payment: Check ☐ Money Order ☐   Do not send cash

Credit Card - May be used for orders over $10.00.   ☐ MC ☐ Visa

Card Exp. Date _____

Card Number _____

Signature _____

Make checks payable to:
Andresen Enterprises
57 Richmond Street
Raynham, MA 02767
Allow 3 weeks for delivery
For quicker delivery call or fax
Phone (508) 821-2550
(800) 749-2550
Fax (508) 821-2550

$6.95 per copy
$1.95 for shipping and handling for first book
Add $.80 shipping for each additional book
Mass. residents add 5% sales tax.

Do you have friends or relatives who would like to have copies of this book? If so, please fill out the order blank below or call to order.

ORDER FORM

Please send _____ copies of MY DADDY DIED at $6.95 each to:

Name _____

Address _____

City _____ State _____ Zip _____

Telephone (_____) _____

Method of payment: Check ☐ Money Order ☐   Do not send cash

Credit Card - May be used for orders over $10.00.   ☐ MC ☐ Visa

Card Exp. Date _____

Card Number _____

Signature _____

Make checks payable to:
Andresen Enterprises
57 Richmond Street
Raynham, MA 02767
Allow 3 weeks for delivery
For quicker delivery call or fax
Phone (508) 821-2550
(800) 749-2550
Fax (508) 821-2550

$6.95 per copy
$1.95 for shipping and handling for first book
Add $.80 shipping for each additional book
Mass. residents add 5% sales tax.

Do you have friends or relatives who would like to have copies of this book? If so, please fill out the order blank below or call to order.

ORDER FORM

Please send _____ copies of MY DADDY DIED at $6.95 each to:

Name _____

Address _____

City _____ State _____ Zip _____

Telephone (_____) _____

Method of payment: Check ☐ Money Order ☐ Do not send cash

Credit Card - May be used for orders over $10.00. ☐ MC ☐ Visa

Card Exp. Date _____

Card Number _____

Signature _____

Make checks payable to:
Andresen Enterprises
57 Richmond Street
Raynham, MA 02767
Allow 3 weeks for delivery
For quicker delivery call or fax
Phone (508) 821-2550
(800) 749-2550
Fax (508) 821-2550

$6.95 per copy
$1.95 for shipping and handling for first book
Add $.80 shipping for each additional book
Mass. residents add 5% sales tax.